D0425689

Jabez, Inc. Copyright 2002
by Gene Swindell and Creative Concepts International, Inc.

Published by:
Creative Concepts International, Inc.
4128 Westchester Crossing
Roswell, GA 30075-1960
www.geneswindell.com

Book Design by Paula Chance

ISBN: 0-9641080-8-9
Printed in the United States of America

Jabez, Inc.

Staff positions available . . .
apply within.

By
Gene Swindell

TABLE OF CONTENTS

FOREWORD

AS SOON AS I COMPLETED READING the manuscript of *Jabez, Inc.*, I realized I was reading something unique. The information in the book made me feel special, like I was part of a bigger plan than I had previously understood. It was like a mystery book unfolding new clues to me. The more I read, the more I wanted to continue to read!

Most books, to me, are either boring or the same old information I have already read, simply repacked in a new and updated edition. This book is different. It is fresh and vibrant, full of life and potential . . . my potential . . . your potential.

Gene Swindell helped me to see that *Jabez, Inc.*, is actually a real business of which I am a part. It is big business, perhaps the biggest business in the world. It is God's business. And if all that is true, and I believe it is, who wouldn't want to be part of that plan?

Whether you realize it or not, *Jabez, Inc.*, has been open for business and in operation for many years. Now is simply our time to be part of all that is taking place. There is a huge business opportunity for you and me to make an investment, the best investment we have ever made. The terms are simple, as you will discover.

I have traveled all over the world. Everywhere I go there seems to be an underlying uneasiness or dissatisfaction with life. There is sort of an attitude of, "Isn't there more to life than what I have experienced so far?" Well, the answer is yes, yes, yes! A thousand times yes! Nothing could be more exciting than to realize Almighty God wants you to be part of His daily plan.

This book will help you see the bigger picture of how you can experience life and fulfillment the way it was intended. What an adventure!

God bless you!

Robert A Rohm Ph.D.
President, Personality Insights, Inc.
Atlanta, Georgia

INTRODUCTION

GLOBAL COMPETITION, rapid-fire changes, increased customer demands, mergers, shrinking profit margins, downsizing, bankruptcies, insider stock trading scandals, and an unstable economy all contribute to the uneasy situations we experience in the world of business today. Executives of corporations as well as owners of small to midsize companies are searching for answers to major challenges that will create competitive advantages in ever-changing markets. Change has replaced status quo in every organization. Customer loyalty has been transferred to competitors offering better quality and faster delivery of products and services. Profits decline as costs increase and prices shrink. Employees face the threat of losing their jobs to continuous downsizing and their 401(K)s in the market slide.

I observe the turmoil and chaos that business

owners, corporate executives, managers and employees face daily in their jobs. Everyone from CEOs and
general managers to salespeople, administrative assistants and maintenance engineers are searching for
stability, security and better results than they've been
getting. Residents in the topsy-turvy world of business
need help.

This bedlam is what inspired me to write this
book. No, I can't reverse economic trends or halt the
instability of the stock market. But _Jabez, Inc._ offers
a business perspective to the short prayer that has
produced long-term results for people worldwide.

At a friend's birthday party, I first heard about
a book titled _The Prayer of Jabez_. Several people that
evening told about the large number of testimonies
that had occurred in the lives of people who had
earnestly prayed Jabez's prayer. A few days later, my
wife Lynn was unexpectedly given a cassette tape of
author Dr. Bruce Wilkinson's Jabez seminar.

We listened to the tape and the next day she
bought the best-seller. I've read the book countless
time and discovered the simple, little prayer is, indeed,
one that will break through to the blessed life. People

in the business world so urgently need its subject today.

Faith is the under girding of this book. I am not a Bible scholar or a minister. I'm a business consultant, seminar leader and speaker, but foremost a Christian, who works with corporations to improve their strategies, productivity and quality. When some friends suggested that I write a corporate application of Jabez, my initial reaction was, "You must be kidding." A feeling of inadequacy suddenly came upon me. I felt totally unqualified to write such a book. How could I assemble the right words, the proper scriptures, and the appropriate stories for such a project? "I can't do it," was my response. And, I went on to explain that, like most business people, there were too many irons in my fire right now — there just would not be enough time to write the book. Then, the words I had read in The *Prayer of Jabez* rang in my ears: *You* can't do it, but *we* can.

I prayed and asked God to bless me, to expand my borders, that His hand would guide me through every word, and that He would protect me from any evil forces that might attempt to interfere. This book is God's message that I am relating. As each word is written, I pray that you will find encouragement and strength to incorporate the prayer of Jabez into your business life and become an effective staff member of the business I call Jabez, Inc.

～

THE JABEZ APPEAL

LET ME EXPLAIN what the prayer of Jabez is all about. The historical records in 1 Chronicles, tracing the family descendants from Adam to Abraham, are a part of the Bible where speed-reading skills can be helpful. The list of Noah's sons, the Hamites, the Semites, descendants of Hagar, Keturah and Sarah, sons of Hezron and Jarahmeelthe, the clans of Caleb, sons of David, the kings of Judah and other tribes of Judah are important but not necessarily interesting reading. Unless you're a Bible scholar or someone inter-ested in ancient genealogy, you probably don't spend a lot of time absorbing 1 Chronicles chapters. Scanning through the first three chapters and moving onto the fourth, the writings become almost a rhythmic pattern.

"To Noah's sons Adam, Seth, Enosh, Kenan, Mahalelel, Jared, etc. Solomon's son was

Rehoboam, Abijah his son, Asa his son,
Jehoshaphat, his son, Jehoram, his son, etc.
etc. . . . The descendants of Judah, Perez,
Hebron, Darmi, Hur and Shobal . . ."

Suddenly, verses nine and ten completely change the cadence of all the other verses.

"Jabez was more honorable than his brothers.
His mother had named him Jabez, saying,
"I gave birth to him in pain." Jabez cried
out to the God of Israel:

"Oh, that you would bless me indeed and
enlarge my territory! Let your hand be with
me, and keep me from evil, so I will not
cause pain.

And God granted his request."

These two verses are like an oasis in the middle of a desert. Verse 11 picks up the cadence again . . . *"Kelub, Shuhah's brother, was the father of Mehir, who was the father of Eshton . . ."* Then, the dramatic impact of that simple request hits.

"And God granted his request!!!" Several exclamation points belong at the end of that sentence.

Here was a man whose mother named him Jabez for the pain she bore in childbirth, he uttered a 28-word prayer and God declared him more honorable and granted his request!

What was the key?

Answer: His simple petition was personal.

He was asking for favor — "Lord, please bless *me*." And he just didn't ask for a small portion. Jabez was asking God to bless him big time — bless me, *indeed*! Sounds rather selfish, doesn't it? No, in fact, it's spiritual. "You do not have, because you do not ask God" *(James 4:2)*.

Many of us have hit a brick wall trying to solve business challenges in searching for some kind of answer to today's turmoil. We have attempted to do it on our own and came up empty. We've followed the advice of so-called business experts, listened to our customers, installed the latest software and applied all the newest management techniques — but nothing works. The time has come to turn elsewhere for a more successful business manual!

Chapter One

BLESS ME GREATLY

"Oh, that You would bless me indeed . . ."

~

Jabez, Inc.

IN BUSINESS, WE LEARN TO BE CAUTIOUS in our pursuits and requests. We calculate the risks. Can we depend on our suppliers to deliver? Will our customers be satisfied? Should we make expenditures for new equipment or expansion in uncertain economic times? Will our customers continue to do business with us? Should we increase or downsize our workforce? Worse case scenarios for these and other questions are discussed every day in corporate boardrooms and backrooms of midsize, small and entrepreneurial companies. Businesspeople are hesitant to act without some guarantee of what to expect.

Can you imagine calling a supplier and placing an open-ended order?

"Hello, ABC Company? This is Joe at XYZ Corporation. I want to place an order. Please send me whatever you think I need. Double or triple the shipment if you think it's necessary. You decide the amount and price. Thanks. Goodbye."

No one in his right mind would place such an order. We want to decide what we want, what price to pay, and when we'll get it. Well, that type of control works in business but the prayer of Jabez reverses the ordering process and requires a step of faith into the unknown. Your request to God for blessings does not contain a purchase order number or an amount desired. There are no quality standards or stock numbers. You are placing an urgent order to God for an overabundance of blessings. He decides what to send, when to deliver, and what price might be attached.

By praying, "bless me indeed," can you expect more business? More revenue? An increase in on-line orders? Better profit-and-loss statements? Fewer challenges? Perhaps. But stop thinking about your personal business desires and start focusing on the business of God.

The prayer of Jabez is not a "quick fix" or a magic wand. It's not a few words that you memorize and just recite every day. It is not a prayer that elevates you above your competition, gives you an unfair advantage or sets you on the path to prosperity. No, the prayer is specifically for God to look upon you favorably with blessings as He sees fit.

When you pray Jabez's prayer, you're asking God

to bless *you*, to expand *your* territories, to guide and to protect *you* from evil. The Lord changes everything based on the *intent* of your prayer. Sure, Jabez asked the Lord to bless him mightily but he didn't specifically request any position of power or number of blessings. He left the distribution up to God to choose what was needed and best for him. Jabez's *intent* was focused on his desire to be *used* by God and was void of selfishness. Yes, he said, "bless *me* indeed." His prayer was not asking God to show favoritism, partiality or take blessings from someone and give them to him.

An act becomes selfish when someone is deprived or hurt by it. For example, you and I work in the same office. Our cubicles are side by side. We both have worked at the ABC Company for about the same length of time and we do similar jobs. The office manager is being promoted to a higher position and the vacancy is going to be filled internally.

If I asked the manager for special favor or manipulated in some manner to be promoted over you and other candidates, this would be selfish. But if I merely told the manager I would like consideration in the search for a replacement, I could accept the position, if offered, guilt free. Asking God to bless you is not a request to pull blessings from someone else. Jabez did what God wanted — to *unselfishly ask* for lots and lots of blessings.

What does it mean to be "blessed?" The Hebrew word means highly favored and fortunate. I believe it also means being kind, happy and successful. Have you ever considered the blessings that flood your life? We fail to take inventory of just how many we enjoy. Jabez wanted an overflow so he added the word "indeed," meaning abundance, profusion and great quantity. He didn't want a single serving — he was begging for an overflowing plateful! And the Lord granted his request, because his intentions were right.

Some people are hesitant — even terrified — to invite God into their lives, let alone into their businesses, fearing what He *might* do. We tend to compartmentalize Him into certain areas and seek His direction in troubling situations or help in times of crisis. Our conversations with Him are like hammering out a business deal. We negotiate and try to force God into agreeing to contractual terms: "Lord, if you'll do point A, I'll do point B." Then, if our request is not fulfilled immediately, we (a) grow impatient, (b) forge ahead to act on our own, and/or (c) fail to recognize (or reject) His answer when it comes.

God wants to bless *you* greatly. He wants to pour out His blessings and change your life but there are a couple conditions:

1. *Recognize that all blessings come from God.* A personnel director might have hired you for the job you now have but that decision actually came from the Lord. A manager might have handed your paycheck to you but the money came from Him. Your last sales contract was approved with a customer's signature, but the name on the bottom line should be been spelled G-O-D. He is the total supplier. "Every good gift and every perfect gift is from above" *(James1:17).*

2. *Ownership of everything must be transferred to God.* No, this is not a merger or acquisition — you relinquish all claims of ownership. God is the CEO, CFO, board of directors and general manager, all in one. Sometimes that means giving up the very possession that is dearest to you. Regardless of position or job, you are the tool

at Jabez, Inc. through which He works.

A business owner sat in a church service reflect-ing on his life. He had amassed millions of dollars from his once-profitable company only to lose it all. In his pocket were two "lucky" coins he had carried for several years. During the service, the offering plate was passed to him. He paused for a moment, then reached into his pocket for one of the coins and placed it in the plate. A few seconds later, he said God spoke to him asking, "Do you trust Me?" He arose from his seat and placed the other coin in the plate.

Later, he started another business and became even wealthier than before. At church functions throughout the area, he testified about his success saying, "everything was given to God. Whether small coins or millions of dollars, He owns them all!"

It's easy to say that God owns everything you have and He supplies your needs, but yet still live as if that were not true. Look at your house and your car. Legal papers show that you (and the lending agency) own those possessions. Yet, honestly adopting Jabez's prayer into your life requires a total change of control. *God **does** own everything*!

In 1976, Tom had a thriving business exporting agriculture products to foreign countries. He was an astute businessman but didn't seek God's guidance in his operations. "I just did things all on my own," he said. Through a series of business mistakes, his business became a financial disaster. Five years later, he lost everything and was completely broke. "God had blessed me but I really messed up," he admitted.

A friend loaned him $600 to buy a used car and he drove to the mountains. Tom decided the time had come for him to ask the Lord to turn things around. In his prayers, he confessed his shortcomings and asked God to bless him with another business.

"I began working as a business broker and was doing well when the idea to develop a cable television system came to me," he explained. "The Lord was telling me, *This is the business I've picked for you. Now, use it as a tool for me.*" Tom took the message seriously. His company began providing cable TV service to one area, then another, and another in various communities throughout the Southeastern states. Over 20 years, the idea evolved into 24 separate cable television systems. As each one grew and became profitable, it was sold to reinvest in other businesses. Today, the highly successful company has moved from establishing and selling cable television systems to reselling telephone services throughout the Southeast.

"God really blessed me," Tom said, "because I turned the business over to Him."

God loves to give and He showers us with unconditional love when we ask. The same Lord who provided food to the children of Israel during the forty years of wandering in the wilderness will supply your needs. Yes, *needs*. The definition of need is a basic necessity of life — food, shelter and clothing. A want is anything beyond a need. God may fulfill our wants but they are His choices.

Perhaps the basic reason we fail to recognize God's role in our lives is our vision of Him. We often shrink God down to fit a human mold with abilities and limitations. The Lord's power and ability is inconceivable to us. He is not some "force" or "wave of energy" that rules over the universe. God is intimately involved with each of us on an individual basis. That's why Jabez prayed, ". . . bless *me*."

The prayer of Jabez is not a petition to God for wealth and affluence, commonly called prosperity gospel. That's an important distinction because so much attention is focused on money in the business world. We're constantly concerned about the bottom line, profit-and-loss statements, annual reports, quarterly profits, margins, expenses, etc. While money is vital to maintain any business, we must consider what God has to say about money. It may surprise you that more than 2,350 verses in the Bible refer to handling money. God's economy, where He plays the central role, is in sharp contrast with man's financial principles. Unless we trust Him with our finances, it's difficult to comprehend God's invisible and supernatural financial system.

In fact, our relationship with the Lord is revealed in how we handle money. "If you have not been trustworthy in handling worldly wealth, who will trust you with true riches?" *(Luke 16:11)*. Yet, the question of why unethical and immoral business people prosper continues to be asked. Perhaps you have become envious of someone who has amassed a fortune through unscrupulous motives. Ungodliness seems to have "paid off" for them. God's blessings should not be equated to prosperity or wealth. His perspective of prosperity is based on a spiritual value system, not on money and possessions. In Revelation 2:9, the godly poor are rich in God's view: "I (the Lord) know your tribulation and your poverty but you are rich." Real prosperity is realized in how closely we follow God's principles. When we do our part in properly handling money within His guidelines, more opportunities are opened to enter into a closer relationship where we find contentment with the Lord.

From my own experience and the testimonies of countless other people in all types of business, here are a couple assurances:

1.   God is sovereign, and you can depend on Him.

2.   He will pour out His blessings when you ask.

The Lord's bounty is not contingent on what position you hold, what school you attended or what business you're in. His blessings sometimes are commensurate with our requests. We simply don't ask to be blessed. Let me suggest that for the next 30 days, pray every day for God to bless *you* — and bless you a *lot*! Pray with expectation and belief that your life will be changed. I can assure you the doors of His warehouse will be opened wide and blessings will continue as long as you ask. God even issues a guarantee: "If you remain in me and my words remain in you, ask whatever you wish, and it will be given you" *(John 15:7)*. Are you ready to be blessed as a staff member of Jabez, Inc.?

YOUR
30-DAY TASK SHEET

1. Every day, write in a journal the blessings God has bestowed on you.

2. Give thanks, and acknowledge that every blessing comes from God.

3. Turn ownership of your possessions over to the Lord.

4. Share your blessings with family, friends, acquaintances and strangers.

5. Open your heart, and enjoy every blessing.

EXPECTED RESULTS

1. Even greater blessings will come from God.

2. An increased dependence on Him will occur.

3. You will have more opportunities to do His work.

4. You will be tested and challenged.

5. The prayer of Jabez will become a part of your daily prayer life.

"Oh, that you would bless me indeed
and enlarge my territory.
That your hand would be with me,
and that you would keep me from evil,
that I may not cause pain."

Chapter Two

WIDEN MY BOUNDARIES

". . . enlarge my territory . . ."

Jabez, Inc.

"MAY I HELP YOU?" That question is asked hundreds of thousands of times each day as receptionists, administrative assistants, customer service representatives and others greet customers on the telephone and face-to-face. These words convey a request to serve. People interacting with customers are encouraged to smile, use a pleasant tone of voice and express a sincere desire to assist. These three important elements set the tone for a cordial conversation and create the first impression every customer has of the company.

In today's highly competitive marketplace, excellent service — personalized to the customer's needs — is often the only thing that differentiates one company from another.

There's more emphasis today on determining the specific needs of each customer so a more customized, personally tailored service program can be designed. Think about the places where you shop — a supermarket, department store, hardware store, dry cleaner, service station and elsewhere. In my neighborhood,

I can choose from a half dozen service stations. I use the one where the attendant is friendly, courteous and remembers my name. You probably return to shops and businesses where you are treated well. Personal service is the name of the game! Every job is a service job. If you're not directly serving customers, you're probably serving someone who is.

The second part of Jabez's prayer . . . *enlarge my territory* . . . is a request to expand your region and create more opportunities where you can serve. Whether you're a top executive or a maintenance engineer, a salesperson or a computer technician, there is a defined area for which you are responsible. Every person who performs a job has a "territory" which could be anything from a geographic region to an office cubicle.

In the business world, we are familiar with Pareto's 80/20 rule. Back in the 17th century, Italian economist Vilfredo Pareto (1848-1923) discovered 80 percent of everything in Italy was owned or controlled by 20% of the population. He later discovered that same ratio was true in other countries and his 80/20 rule has become a universal principle. For example, salespeople get 80 percent of their business from 20 percent of their customers. In business meetings, 80 percent of decisions are made by 20 percent of those attending. At your office, 80 percent of the mess is in 20 percent of your work area. It's a principle of life!

In your "territory," you probably are comfortable in the center of that area — the 80 percent. You know most of your associates and customers pretty well, everything remains status quo and you enjoy the regular routine. In fact, that is your "comfort capsule." It feels good because there is little or no change. But out in the 20 percent range where the terrain is unfamiliar, things are different. That part of your territory is a bit uncomfortable because you encounter resistant people identified by Dr. Bruce Wilkinson as "Border Bullies." These individuals outside your comfort zone delight in criticizing, judging and disapproving. They are the ones who exert great effort to confine you to the warm and fuzzy portion of your comfort zone.

And now, as if you didn't have enough challenges with the "Bullies" in your current space, you are supposed to pray for *more* territory? Yes. It's like the Texas rancher who didn't want *all* the land, just the areas that border *his* property. Your prayer may or may not be answered with more land, property or room for yourself. Your plea should be for more blessings of confidence and peace in not only your 20 percent area but beyond those borders to focus on even more people in ever-increasing territories that can be claimed as God's dominion. Yes, perhaps even more resistance will be poured forth but for you to remain in your "comfort capsule" is to stagnate. God wants you to go far beyond your borders.

There are people who are very content in their own little comfort areas. Oh, they talk about how everyone should reach out and help others but when they're asked to *do* something, they find a dozen excuses. These people are more interested in voicing words of concern in their staid comfort capsules than using God's power to change lives and gain eternal results.

Moses came up with lots of excuses when God urged him to leave his comfort zone. "Then Moses said to the Lord, "Oh my Lord, I am not eloquent, neither in the past nor since You have spoken to your servant. I am slow of speech and tongue." God replied, "Who gave man his mouth? Who makes him deaf or mute? Who gives him sight or makes him blind? Is it not I, the Lord? Now go; I will help you speak and teach you what to say." But Moses persisted, "O my Lord, please send someone else to do it" *(Exodus 4:10-13)*. God was nudging him out of status quo.

Managers face this problem with employees. For example, Helen had worked as a research assistant at a chemical lab in a major corporation for eight years. She was dependable and showed great potential. A technician's position became available and she was offered the spot but she would be required to get more education. The company agreed to pay tuition for her to attend classes two nights a week at the local university for four months.

Helen first said she didn't feel qualified to be considered. The lab chief assured her that she was the best candidate. He further said the number of staff assistants was being reduced and there was a possibility her job would be cut. He advised her to take the offer. Despite the chief's encouragement, Helen had another excuse: she didn't want to commit to four months of schooling. It was obvious Helen was cozy in her comfort zone and, despite the opportunity and warning, she wanted to remain immobile. Six weeks later the staff was downsized and she lost her job.

The only thing that remains status quo in God's world is God. His promises remain unchanged. The Lord wants you to ask for more territory, then show up for work. He will do the rest. But remember the *intent* of your prayer — expansion not for your reasons but for His purpose. It is important that you remember the fact that God is not primarily focused on changing your circumstances. He is primarily focused on changing your heart! And it will be through the expansion of your territory that this "heart change" will occur.

Salespeople should be seeking larger territories, not for potential increases in sales and bigger commission checks, but for greater opportunities to share God's love through interaction with customers. Accountants and service reps should be asking for expanded areas outside their workstations and cubicles. Marketing people, designers, and engineers need to pray for enlarged boundaries where God can use them.

Regardless of your job, the prayer to expand your territory is a plea to give you more space in which to minister. In your larger territory, He will give you new opportunities for *Jabez Moments.*

A JABEZ MOMENT

God creates Jabez Moments. Our job is to recognize these times and take appropriate action.

Joe, a salesman, and I flew to Dallas for a full day of business appointments a few years ago. After our last meeting, we ate dinner and drove to the airport for our flight back to Atlanta. At the gate, we learned the 8:30 flight was delayed for two hours due to a mechanical problem with the plane. Joe and I sat down and began discussing the day's meetings and follow-up calls we would make to clients later that week. Our conversation later moved on to the day's news, sports and things that were happening in our lives. Joe had never openly discussed his personal life with me before. As we continued to talk, he began revealing some recent marital problems. He said there had been little communication with his wife in recent weeks and their differences had grown to where they were barely speaking. He said divorce was a strong possibility.

I listened as Joe poured out his problems. Then, I asked if there was anything I could do to help. He sat in silence staring at the floor. I asked if he had turned to God for help. He shook his head. I shared some personal experiences how the Lord had miraculously resolved issues in my life through prayer. Then I asked Joe if he would like to pray for God's help. He paused for a moment, but then declined. He thanked me, opened up a newspaper and began reading. I didn't say another word but silently prayed for the Lord to help Joe and his wife with their problems. We finally boarded the plane and headed to Atlanta, hardly saying anything to each other enroute.

It was 1:30 a.m. when Joe got out of my car, waved goodbye and walked to the front door of his house. As I continued driving, my thoughts reflected back to the problems he had revealed. Again, I said a small prayer as I got into bed and fell asleep. At 6:30 a.m., the telephone ringing awakened me. I picked up the receiver and it was Joe calling. He quickly apologized for calling so early. He said he wanted to share some good news. When he returned home at that early hour, his wife was awake and they began talking about some of the issues in their marriage. He said it was the first in-depth conversation in their ten-year marriage. After awhile, Joe suggested that they pray together for God's help.

"The conversation we had in Dallas got me thinking. I appreciated your concern but I really wanted to talk with my wife, and then pray with her for God's help. We're going to get our marriage back together. I just wanted you to know. Thanks." he said.

Too often we separate our spiritual and secular business lives. There are many who feel that one church service is sufficient to carry them through the week. The seven-day gap is filled with negotiating deals, selling products and satisfying customers. With our busy schedules, there never seems to be enough time to get everything done. Chinese Author Watchman Nee wrote about "the things in the hand." He suggests we hold things loosely in our hands. In other words, don't cram your schedule so full that when God gives you something else to hold or to carry, you don't have to ask Him to wait while you juggle all those things to make room for His request, or you have to find a place to carefully lay it down till later.

Bringing God into your life is a 24/7/365 arrangement that closes the weeklong Monday thru Saturday spiritual gap. There are always jobs available and excellent training in the Lord's workforce at Jabez, Inc. "I will instruct you and teach you in the way you should go; I will counsel you and watch over you" *(Psalm 32:8)*. Not surprisingly, God works miracles through un-trained spiritual representatives. In fact, he prefers someone willing to be a spiritually anointed messenger rather than a self-appointed conveyor of information. When you pray for expansion of your territory, be open to His leading to speak the words and take the actions necessary at that precise moment . . . *a Jabez Moment.*

Sheryl purchased a small antique shop in 1999 and was very excited about the revenues that came in during the first three months. She decided to expand the shop and leased adjoining rooms. Business tripled over the next six months, more staff was hired and she was spending more and more time each day at the shop. A few months ago, she started praying Jabez's prayer but each time she said the words, *enlarge my territory*, her mind quickly registered: *cancel, I have too much space already*. Regardless, she continued to pray each day but with her business perspective, not God's purpose.

A customer in the shop told her about a Bible study group that needed a central location to meet each week. Sheryl was asked if the shop could be the meeting place. Her first reaction was there would not be enough space for a large group of people to assemble. Then, she looked at one corner of her shop where several rail back chairs were displayed and she began visualizing how they could be arranged in a semicircle. She figured 12, maybe 15, could be comfortably seated. She would open the shop doors at 7 a.m. each Friday for the Bible study group, she would serve coffee and donuts but the group would have to be confined to 15. She contacted the customer and announced her decision.

On the first Friday morning, 10 people attended. The next week 13, then 16, then 20. Each week more people showed up and Sheryl scrambled to find more chairs and expand the territory. Before long, nearly 40 people attended each week, including the entire antique store staff. Meanwhile, Sheryl's business continued to grow to where the corner area was needed to display more antiques. But she refused to give up that space. Instead, she placed a sign in that section: *This area permanently reserved for a weekly Bible study. Come join us — there's always room for you.* Each Friday morning, people assemble there in Sheryl's expanded territory.

Just as you are expected to be productive in the space where you're employed, God holds you responsible for your productivity as a Jabez, Inc. staff member. Greater commitment and service bring bigger blessings and spiritual rewards. Call it ROI — return on investment.

Luke 19:13-26 relates the story of a noble man who was to be appointed king in a distant country. Before his journey, he called ten of his servants and gave ten minas, about three month's wages, to each one. He instructed them to put the money to work until he returned. When he returned as king, he summoned the servants to find out what they had gained

with the money. The first reported the mina had
returned ten more. "Well done, my good servant, his
master replied. "Because you have been trustworthy
in a very small matter, take charge of ten cities. The
second came and reported the mina had earned five
more. His master answered, "You take charge of five
cities." Then another servant came and returned the
original mina explaining it had been kept in a piece of
cloth. "Why didn't you put my money on deposit, so
that when I came back, I could have collected it with
interest?" the master asked. Then he ordered the mina
taken away from the servant and given to the one
who had ten. When questioned about his decision,
he replied, "I tell you that to everyone who has, more
will be given, but as for the one who has nothing,
even what he has will be taken away."

Throughout the scriptures, handling of money
is regarded as the true index to a person's character.
There is a correlation between the development of
character and how a person handles money. David
McConaugh, in his book *Money The Acid Test*, says,
"Money, most common of temporal things, involves
uncommon and eternal consequences. Even though it

may be done quite unconsciously, money molds men in the process of getting it, saving it, spending it and giving it. Depending on how you use it, it proves to be a blessing or a curse to its possessor. Either the person becomes master of the money or the money becomes master of the person. He takes money, as essential as it is to our common life, and as sordid as it sometimes seems, and makes it a touchstone to test the lives of men and an instrument to mold people into the likeness of Himself."

There's a story about a man who died and arrived at the Heaven's gate with a suitcase. St. Peter opened the gate for him to enter and asked him to leave the suitcase behind. The man said he must take the suitcase with him to show God what he accomplished in his time on earth. St. Peter opened the case and looked inside and found two gold bars.

"You can see why it's so important to bring these along," the man said. St. Peter looked puzzled and asked, "Why are you bringing in PAVEMENT?" There's a vast difference between what we value verses what God values.

Every individual is given skills, talents and

money that can be utilized in their expanded territory.
A marketing executive who designs a promotional
campaign that increases sales by 50 percent can use
his skills to boost church attendance 50 percent. A
salesperson that talks with customers every day has
countless opportunities as a messenger of God's word.
An office worker, a service rep, an engineer, a supervisor, a line worker — everyone can use their gifts and
funds when they become a member of the Jabez, Inc.
staff. He just wants you to apply for the job through
prayer. As you begin working and your territory
becomes larger, there will be more opportunities for
your span of service to increase even more.

HOW TO
ENLARGE YOUR TERRITORY

1. Ask God consistently to expand the borders of your territory.

2. Be ready to act upon every possible Jabez moment.

3. Prepare to overcome the "Border Bullies" in your territory.

4. Allow God to use your skills and abilities for His work.

5. Expect the Lord to do great works through you.

> *"Do not store up for yourselves treasures on earth, where moth and rust destroy, and where thieves break in and steal. But store up for yourselves treasures in heaven, where moth and rust do not destroy, and where thieves do not break in and steal.*
>
> *For where your treasure is, there your heart will be also."*

Matthew 6:19-21

Chapter Three

GOD'S DIRECTION

"Oh, that Your hand would be with me . . ."

~

Jabez, Inc.

SELF-DOUBT AND FEAR OF FAILURE are two of the greatest barriers we face in our lives. When confronted with decisions, we often feel uninformed, unqualified and unwilling to take risks. We often play the procrastination game called *"What if . . ."* *What if* I make the wrong choice? *What if* I go in the wrong direction? *What if* I make a major mistake? *What if* people don't agree with me? These questions do two things:

1. Sink your confidence level, and

2. Allow a feeling of fear to take over.

Perhaps you are at this point and questioning whether Jabez's prayer will work for you. *What if* I ask God for a tremendous amount of blessings in a wider territory, can I handle the Jabez moments that are bound to come? *What if* I get into a situation that is beyond my knowledge or experience? *What if* things don't work out the way I planned?

Good. You're normal and now thinking like Jabez!

His prayer was one of desperation because his

life was destined for scorn and ridicule. Remember, his mother named him for the pain she suffered in giving birth. Imagine being introduced to someone . . . *"I would like you to meet Jabez"* . . . and that person quickly walked away without a handshake. Not many people would want to associate with a guy whose moniker meant pain! He needed help!

There are two inner "voices" that speak to us. One is the gentle voice of God that conveys hope, encouragement, comfort and confidence. The other is the deceptive voice of the discourager that speaks doubt, apprehension, anxiety and fear. These messages come in the form of thoughts. When the gentle voice of God says, "go forth and do My work," the arrogant voice of the evil one quickly responds, "you can't do that."

Has there been a time when you failed to speak or act because of fear or feeling incapable? The discouraging voice probably began whispering, then became louder and louder until it was shouting . . . "YOU CAN'T DO IT." The negative thoughts pounded away until you finally surrendered and gave in. We've all experienced times when our fears held us captive. Fear is best described as

False

Evidence

Appearing

Real

. . . a mirage, a delusion . . . when situations appear overwhelming, problems are too great and you feel inadequate. These are times to focus and concentrate on the reassuring thoughts from God that will crush the feeling of fear and uncertainty. "Listen, my son, and be wise, and keep your heart on the right path" (*Proverbs 23:19*).

A few years ago, one of my clients had a struggle over whether to expand his operations. After working several years in a major electronics corporation, Doug opened a small circuit board manufacturing plant. Stepping from the secure corporate surroundings into the fearful entrepreneurial world was frightening. He asked God to give him wisdom and guidance in the new venture. The business grew slowing for the first two years, and then some major orders for immediate turnaround exceeded his production capability. He subcontracted a portion of the jobs to meet deadlines.

A few weeks passed and another deluge of orders came in, then another wave, and another. He faced a major decision whether to continue in the same location and continue subcontracting when necessary, or move to a larger facility. He prayed and felt God was leading him to expand but each time he considered costs or location, fears would mount to where he would abandon the idea. One afternoon, Doug left the plant and drove to quiet spot near a lake. He spent two hours just praying and asking the Lord to help him overcome those negative thoughts. When he returned to the plant, Doug said he had peace that he had never experienced before. He felt confident that God's direction was to move forward. Two years have passed since the new plant was built and business has tripled.

Count on a deluge of negative "you can't" messages to begin once you join God's workforce. That's why the words of Jabez . . . *"that your hand would be with me"*. . . is so important to give you strength and assurance. But there must be a measure of common sense on your part as well.

A high wire circus performer worked without a net, because he believed God would always protect him from harm. When asked about his death-defying movements on a thin wire hundreds of feet in the air, the aerialist would reply, "God is able to keep me from falling." What did his carelessness about his own life suggest about his view of life? A motorist doesn't deliberately drive a car off a mountain cliff and say the Lord will miraculously reach down and bring the car back to safe ground. God is not obligated to protect anyone from poor choices, consequences . . . and gravity?

God wants you to be self-confident. The term does not mean self-centered or self-absorbed. Self-confidence does not equal pride and arrogance. Self-confidence is competence through knowledge, poise and focus, rooted in Him. We know that in Him, we will not be put to shame. Self-confidence demands self-discipline and it is built on your ability to assemble the full God-given resources of mind, body and spirit to handle any challenge . . . *with His direction*!

Mark, an electrical contractor, was asked to help a small church in its building project. With a heavy workload, he agreed to oversee the project and do a small part of the technical work. After a short time, he realized the project would be better served if he and his one employee would do the complete job. Mark realized there would be a major problem in finding time to get the church project completed on time while fulfilling their other work obligations. He prayed that God would give him insight into how he could schedule all the work that had to be done.

The Lord worked everything out. Mark's donation to the church's new children center amounted to nearly $45,000 in materials and labor and not a single business appointment was missed during that time. In fact, additional business came in so that not a penny was lost. One month later, Mark received a contract to do electrical work for a contracting company that builds communication buildings. His company now has seven employees, and billings have gone from $8,000 per month to averaging $8,000 to $10,000 per week. Mark's prayers brought an overflow of blessings, and he has expanded his contributions for several Christian projects. "I gave God the keys to my business to run it as he saw fit," Mark explains.

"When I find myself in a perplexing situation, I just say, 'It's yours . . . what do you want me to do?' "

God's hand is becoming increasingly visible in the business world today. The movement to join God's workforce is being seen in corporate headquarters, offices and plants everywhere. Business people are rising early to attend Bible studies, lunchtime prayer groups are meeting in restaurants and others are getting together with their spouses in evening sessions. On several fronts, people are rejecting the idea that spirituality cannot mix with commerce. They refuse to believe that their jobs are mundane and meaningless. In fact, businesspeople in many parts of the world are being challenged to become messengers and distributors of God's love in the marketplace.

In a New York City lecture series, Dr. Thomas K. Tewell asked, "Are you willing to be a channel in the divine economy?" David W. Miller, a former IBM executive and investment banker, lectures on "everyday Christianity" explaining that "God is found in earth and rocks and buildings and institutions, and, yes, in the business world." Miller, who founded The Avodah (a Hebrew word that means both work and worship) Institute, says "There's a great hunger among business people and professionals to find meaning in their work, to discover significance in their success, and to live more spiritual lives. Many find it difficult to align actions with beliefs, due to a tension between marketplace pressures and faith principles. People often keep faith and work in separate compartments, resulting in a personal sense of dislocation and disintegration. Many business, educational, and religious institutions are unsure how to respond. Our goal is to help change all that by providing information, ideas, events, and a repository of knowledge and understanding on the issues surrounding the integration of faith and work."

In the July 9, 2001 issue of *Fortune* magazine, author Marc Gunther wrote:

> "The spiritual revival in the workplace reflects, in part, a broader religious reawakening in America, which remains one of the world's most observant nations. (Depending on how the question is asked, as many as 95% of Americans say they believe in God; in much of Western Europe, the figure is

closer to 50%.) The Princeton Religious
Research Index, which has tracked the
strength of organized religion in America
since World War II, reports a sharp increase
in religious beliefs and practices since the
mid-1990's. When the Gallup Poll asked
Americans in 1999 if they felt a need to
experience spiritual growth, 78% said yes,
up from 20% in 1994; nearly half said
they'd had occasion to talk about their faith
in the workplace in the past 24 hours."

Have you ever felt God's hand upon you? I
don't mean physically touching your shoulder but
you realized there was divine guidance and direction.
Have you ever made a decision and then realized, as
you looked back with 20/20 hindsight, that He guided
you to that choice. There have been times in my life
that I knew for certain the Lord had his hand on me.
In business situations where I have both received contracts and lost accounts, I can look back in retrospect
and realize God controlled those transactions.

Recently, I made a proposal to a large corporation to do a series of workshops over a period of

several months. The contract would be for several thousand dollars. From all indications, the decision makers were pleased with the proposal and ready to sign on the bottom line. Then came a phone call advising me that another company with a lower bid had been given the contract. I was puzzled and asked if my proposal might be modified to fit their budget. The answer was, "No the contract is being signed today." Six months later, the corporation filed for bankruptcy and its creditors were left holding the bag.

God directs and protects. The "hand of God" that Jabez sought was the Lord's supernatural guidance upon his life. Sometimes, as humans, we question His actions and interventions only to learn later that our way would have been disastrous. There are times when God's hand seems to have disappeared — we pray for direction but the answers don't come and we immediately start rationalizing our desires rather than wait for His will to come forth. Perhaps our prayer should be for more patience and peace. Rest assured, when you ask for God's hand to be with you, He will _never_ leave you. Through *His* hand comes the power with which you perform the Lord's work.

A young marketing director was not given a contract that had been expected, promised, deserved and earned. An associate listened to him complain about his disappointment and then replied, "Don't worry. It's just a 'stone job' anyhow. What you think of now as 'bread' will eventually become 'stone' and you could break your teeth trying to chew it." These wise words came true only a few months later when the once-prized contract became a corporate disaster.

Jesus asked, "What father, if his child asked for bread, would give him a stone, or if he asked for fish would give him a serpent? If you, being evil, know how to give good gifts to your children, how much more will your heavenly Father give good gifts to those who ask him?" (*Luke 7:11*). The Lord knew what the young marketing director didn't know. The hand of God kept him from the stone and gave him bread instead.

In the chaotic world of business, *peace* is almost a foreign word. People are in a fast-paced fury headed from one catastrophe to another. At day's end, the soles of our shoes are scorched from extinguishing crises all day. The enemies of peace work overtime.

Selfishness, power struggles, poor communication, bad behavior and jealousy keep us on edge. Peace is absent in our world of clamor. There's an inner peace that comes in the midst of turmoil when we really know Him and fully realize His hand is upon us. "And the peace of God, which transcends all understanding, will guard your hearts (emotions) and your minds (thoughts) in Christ" (Philippians 4:7). God brings a three-fold peace: peace *with* God, peace *of* God and peace *with* others.

The power that comes to us through God's hand brings a sense of godliness. When we yield to His leading, astonishing things happen. People, who were never open to share their thoughts before, now are eager to converse with you. Challenges that once appeared impossible are erased. Doors that were once closed are opened. The supernatural power of God working through you is miraculous. But herein lies a potential problem. Godliness can become an obstruction in the Lord's pipeline of power. For someone to take credit for God's work is misrepresenting the source. It's like a fellow employee accepting a bonus for your accomplishment. Don't ever forget that it's *His* power, not yours. And, *His* power is not increased through *your* religious activities or good intentions. Only through *His* hand can you experience Jabez Moments.

An experience that brought me to a sudden awakening that God's hand was, indeed, upon my life occurred one night during my ten years as a broadcaster and speaker for General Motors Corporation. On a Saturday in May, I had worked in Anderson, Indiana, where GM had two major plants, as emcee at a big variety show that was part of the town's annual springtime festival. After the show, the musical conductor from New York City asked me to drive him to the Indianapolis airport for a late night flight. GM had provided me with a new Cadillac and I volunteered to make the 50-mile drive.

It was nearly midnight when I dropped him off at the airport and headed back to Anderson. As I left the city, my eyes began to get heavy. I turned up the volume on the radio, opened the windows to let the night air blow on my face and sat straight in the seat. But despite my efforts, I fell asleep a short distance out of the city. I was awakened suddenly as the speeding car left the pavement and the wheels ran onto gravel. Only a few feet in front of me was a road sign and the car was headed directly toward it. I instinctively turned the steering wheel sharply to the left and the car spun out of control. The tires were screeching as I made a complete circle on the roadway and stopped on the opposite side, headed in the other direction.

My heart was pounding as I sat there in shock. It took a few minutes for me to realize what had happened. Considering the speed at which I suddenly swerved, only a miracle kept the car from going completely off the highway, rolling over in that wild spin or crashing into oncoming traffic.

There's only one answer: God had his hand on me that night. One of my favorite passages is "Trust in the Lord with all your heart and lean not on your own understanding; in all your ways acknowledge Him and He will make your paths straight" (*Proverbs 3:5-6*).

As God directs and guides you, humble yourself under His powerful hand and focus your efforts on accomplishing the things He wants done. He will work in you, to do His will and to do His good pleasure. As a staff member of Jabez, Inc., there's plenty of work you can do. The Lord just wants you to show up!

The story of Moses in Exodus is a great example. When God sent Moses to deliver the children of Israel from Egypt, Moses said, "I don't have an army. I don't have any equipment. I don't have the things it takes to conquer a kingdom."

God asked Moses, "What do you have in your hand?" "A shepherd's rod," Moses replied.

"Throw it down on the ground," God instructed him. Moses threw the rod down, and it became a hissing serpent. Then God said, "Grab it by the tail." Moses carefully reach down, grabbed the snake by the tail and it became a rod in his hand again. God said, "That's all you will need. Go down and deliver my people from Egypt . . . and use what you've got."

There's no need to wait until everything is in place or your schedule is more flexible to ask God's hand to be placed upon you. Regardless of your personal or professional circumstances, He's waiting now for you to ask. Then, He will direct your path.

HOW TO FEEL
THE HAND OF GOD

1. Ask and receive God's direction and protection.

2. Experience His power expanding beyond your abilities.

3. Gain wisdom through Him to face inevitable challenges.

4. Don't take credit for anything — remember, it's His power.

5. Just show up and let God work through you.

"I will instruct you and teach you in the way you should go; I will counsel you and watch over you."

Psalm 32:8

Chapter Four

DIVINE PROTECTION

" . . . keep me from evil . . ."

THE CEO OF A LARGE CORPORATION recently talked about how his faith intertwines with the tough ethical and commercial decisions he makes every day. He said the importance of doing the "next right thing" takes top priority in every decision he considers — even over the cost of his decision. The gentleman is convinced that if costs are the primary consideration, the numbers will invariably distort the decision. He went on to explain that, of course, costs have to be calculated but not during the decision process. The unwritten rule in his corporation is never to ask, "how much does it cost?" while considering a decision in any given crisis. There are undoubtedly challenges from the "bean-counting" accountants but the top executive believes that if you set a numbers-driven tone, you corrupt people and apply too much pressure on managers. He is living proof that one can uphold Christian values in business.

Headlines of business mismanagement, insider trading deals, executive greed, and accounting negligence clearly point out the depths to which corporate

America has fallen. Workshops are being conducted on ethics and moral principles. Does that say something about our society? Having to teach people to be honest, trustworthy and do the "next right thing" is shocking!

On the other hand, we should not be surprised. Temptations to stray away from God's path abound in the world of business. Just ask the former employees of Enron.

Recently, I was to speak at a conference in southern New Jersey and reserved a rental car to make the one-hour drive from Newark airport. A representative of the sponsoring organization met me at the terminal to ride to the hotel and return the following day. When we returned the next afternoon, I received a receipt for the rental car charges to my credit card. The sales rep then asked the rental agent to make him a copy "for his file." He turned to me and whispered, "I turn it in on my expense account." When I questioned his honesty, he explained the practice is common in his company. Where's his conscience?

Jabez was a wise man. He knew with the Lord's blessings in a larger territory, he would need even more protection from evil. Sure, God's hand would be with him but he knew temptations would increase and become even stronger. When your blessings come and you start working for God, watch out! Enemy No. 1 lurks in the darkness. Once you begin to invade his territory, he fights back by tempting and tantalizing in every way possible.

For many years, I've been a road warrior — a businessperson who spends lots of time in airplanes, airports, automobiles, hotels and restaurants. Temptations hide in many places.

Every hotel room has a television set promoting adult movies; porno sites are available on a laptop computer in the privacy of your room; a lobby bar has people looking for love in all the wrong places, and nearby adult clubs use neon and nudity to entice customers into a pit of sin. Without strong spiritual commitments, there are massive enticements labeled as exciting pleasures that travelers can easily stumble into. Some succumb to the lure and attempt to keep their dark sins secret. But, consequences are always inevitable.

Temptations are widespread in offices, manufacturing plants and other places of business, too. Opportunities for extramarital or illicit affairs abound. Men and women, who work in the same organization or meet through business connections, fall into immoral relationships that destroy marriages and self-respect. There are temptations to impulsively steal, cheat and falsify documents, as well as the increasing problems that drugs and drinking cause in the workplace. There's a false perception that the secret is safe but each person who falls victim to temptation has to deal with his or her own conscience.

Yes, it's a jungle out there! And it's a jungle "in here" when one knows their heart to be deceitful and wicked.

It's easy to claim ignorance, calling it *innocence*, when we sin. The next time we trust our *innocence*, we call it *victimized*. So-called *"innocent victims"* recoil when they hear the words of God, "Those things which proceed out of the mouth come from the heart; for out of the heart proceed evil thoughts, murders, adulteries, fornications, thefts, false witness, blasphemies. These are the things which defile a man" (*Matthew 15:18-20*). In other words, it is not the things on the outside that get us into trouble. It is the things in our own heart that lead us astray. The "*victims*" resent what He reveals, saying, "I never felt any of those terrible things in my heart." Either the Lord is the supreme expert on the human heart or He is a fraud. He knows every heart that directs the mind and the mouth. The "*victims*" are living in a fool's paradise. It all comes down to a choice: trust that God will protect us from the evil inside of our own hearts or trust our own judgment when temptations beckon. My vote goes to Him!

There are three "powers" connected to every job. Regardless of the tasks performed and level of authority, these three elements are evident.

• First, there's skill power — the talents and abilities to do the job.

• Second, knowledge power — experience and know-how.

• Third, position power — the influence attached to a job or position.

Everyone holding a job has varying degrees of all three powers.

For some people, skill and knowledge powers create barriers in their communications and relationships with others. When I work in the high tech industry, there are times I need an interpreter to understand the language. With their brilliant minds, the technicians, scientists and engineers clearly understand the world of bytes, megabytes, semiconductors, biotechnology and telecoms where I'm a total stranger.

With position power, some people rule over those in lower levels of authority. Top executives or managers might show disrespect or favoritism while others might display arrogant behaviors to appear superior. Employees with more seniority in a company might seek to better themselves at the expense of people with less employment time. Power plays are common in our daily business lives. In fact, I jokingly believe maintenance engineers use their position power when they place those yellow signs at rest room doors: ROOM CLOSED FOR CLEANING. That's Don Juan of the John power!

In addition to these three powers, there is one more element, *the most important*, to every job — God's power! Asking God to erect a "hedge of protection" around you makes a tremendous difference in your life. His protection will not mean you will be void of sin in your personal life or the struggles in your professional career. His promise is to provide an escape route from *temptation* to sin.

In its original sense, to sin meant "missing the mark" when archers failed to shoot their arrows into the center of their targets. When an archer would miss the mark, he would take closer aim and fire again and again, each time striving for perfection. God's power in our lives will check us when we're tempted to abuse our skills, knowledge and position powers and drive off target. When we depend on Him for protection, the allure of transgression is diverted, removed or eliminated. Our prayer is for God to free us and keep us from temptations of pride, envy, lying, lust, greed and countless other sins each day.

If the Lord gives you a leadership role, use your position discreetly — for Him. We're all sinners but He tells us to confess our sins to be forgiven and cleansed from all unrighteousness. "If we claim we have not sinned, we make him out to be a liar and his word has no place in our lives" (*1 John 1:10*).

Psalm 91 gives the details of God's protection. "Because he loves me," says the Lord, "I will rescue him; I will protect him, for he acknowledges my name. He will call upon me, and I will answer him; I will be with him in trouble, I will deliver him and honor him" (*Verses 14-15*).

He does not give us overcoming power. He gives us supernatural power as we overcome our adversities and begin living like Jabez — being grateful for bountiful blessings, expanded territory, His guiding hand and protection each day.

GETTING GOD'S PROTECTION FROM EVIL

1. Pray daily for God to protect and keep you from evil.

2. Ask Him to keep you from sin.

3. If there is a specific sin that troubles you, ask Him to remove it from you life.

4. Acknowledge and give thanks for His mercy in giving you protection.

5. Realize that your daily actions have a direct effect on the lives of other people.

"Watch and pray, lest you enter into temptation. The spirit indeed is willing, but the flesh is weak."

Matthew 26:41

Chapter Five

I Do Not Want to Intentionally Hurt Anyone

" . . . that I may not cause pain."

❧

Jabez, Inc.

QUESTION: On most manager's and supervisor's "to do" list, what is lower than cleaning up toxic waste spills? Answer: Performance reviews.

No one likes to pull out the files on each employee, prepare a review, schedule an hour for each person, then go through the routine of evaluating their performance over the past six months or year. Most leaders delay performance reviews until the last minute, because they're associated with conflict, confrontation and all things negative. The hour-long reviews usually turn out to be a manager's subjective opinion vs. the employee's biased view. Many times harsh words are exchanged that slash like a knife into the heart of each person. If only managers, supervisors and employees alike could learn to be considerate and tactful.

There is so much pain in the business world, a place sometimes referred to as a "dog-eat-dog" arena. Every transaction must be scrutinized carefully in fear of a lawsuit. Competition among companies has become fierce and sometimes the "good guys," who do business above the table, don't win. Contracts and orders are altered and corners are unethically cut to gain advantage, then rationalized as "just the way we do business today." Employees no longer trust their employer and vise versa. Evil abounds in many corners of the marketplace.

The last request in Jabez's prayer — "*. . .that I may not cause pain*" — calls me to reflect on my life. I wonder how many people have suffered pain from my words and actions? Looking back over the years, I'm certain there are many more wounds than my mind can recall because so often, the pain suffered by another person is overlooked or it goes unannounced. Sure, I can remember major conflicts and confrontations where words were spoken or actions taken that undoubtedly caused pain to someone. In many of those instances, I offered an apology. But in others, I did not because, at that moment, the incident didn't appear that hurtful. My prayer now is for forgiveness.

Each one of us has experienced painful situations that are regrettable, even some that were unavoidable. With downsizing and restructuring in so many organizations, top executives are forced to make layoff decisions that affect many lives — not just dismissed employees' but their family members' as well.

The personnel director in the headquarters of a huge telecommunications corporation where I visited recently was deeply concerned over the layoff of several hundred employees that day. The loss of a paycheck also impacts stores and businesses that depend on the employees' spending each week. Although painful to the administrator and the recipient, economic conditions sometimes demand drastic action for corporate survival — but that still doesn't ease the pain. We need God's help in these matters.

The rampant sin of sexual immorality, mentioned in the previous chapter, is causing incredible pain among businesspeople today. The "live for the moment" lifestyle that has invaded our society snares both married and single people into decadent relationships that ultimately wind up causing pain, not only for the participants but spouses, families and friends as well. And many of these wounds become permanent scars. There also are instances when sharp words and rude behavior inflict severe pain. At the time, these occasions are minimized because they are considered a "slip of the tongue" or acts in the "heat of the moment" but still, wounds have been inflicted. We underestimate the lasting pain that our sins cause to ourselves, to others and, most of all, to God.

As a young high school student in my hometown of Alexandria, Indiana, I worked in a local grocery store after school. The manager was a "leave-alone-ZAP" type of guy — he never offered any praise but was quick to lash out at an employee who made a mistake. When I arrived for work one afternoon, he instructed me to go to the back room, get ten crates of head lettuce, trim off the brown leaves, place them back in the crates and return them to the cooler. I found a sharp knife and began the trimming. The manager walked into the back room at the exact moment I was trimming the last head of lettuce and I got ZAPPED! The once large eight-inch heads of lettuce had been reduced to small four-inch size. Every leaf with a brown spot had been cut off. I became the target of his wrath for doing what he asked — trim off the brown leaves — a mistake that brought volatile consequences. Although I've forgiven him, his painful words still ring in my ears.

Jabez had a good reason to ask God to keep him from causing pain to others. Just the mention of his name brought a warning that he could bring suffering. Your name and mine might not reflect pain but our prayer should resound just as loudly as Jabez's. We need moment-to-moment reminders to throttle our overly aggressive behaviors and offensive, discourteous remarks. In other words, "cool it."

Before Lynn and I were married, we made a vow to exhort each other, to avoid criticizing and speaking harshly. Bitter words are like permanent wounds in the brain. Yes, we have occasional disagreements, but never to the point of raging anger where words and actions can leave irreparable pain.

Pride is often a source of pain. In my seminars, I often speak about pride — being proud of your job, your workmanship, your efforts, your company, your loyalty and dedication to your employer. There's nothing wrong with having a feeling of pride and self-worth as long as it's balanced with humility. So many people excel in their work to the point of becoming arrogant and conceited. Sometimes a promotion to a higher position, an award for outstanding work or a bonus received for the largest sales increase causes a person to take on an air of self-importance. They get a bad case of what I call "pride power." Their haughty attitude takes them over the edge and, despite their outstanding accomplishments; pride prevents them from finding God's real purpose for them in their lives. "Pride goes before destruction, and a haughty spirit before a fall" (*Proverbs 16:18*).

Beware of adopting a lifestyle of "pride power" once you start working at Jabez, Inc. The power that God bestows upon you is given for His work, not yours. Although He promises that *through* Him you can do great works, credit still goes to the Lord. People who claim *they* performed miracles or *they* were responsible for leading someone out of despair trouble me. We are nothing — but *with* the Lord, we can do anything. And to Him goes the glory!

God wants us to be compassionate. "But I tell you who hear me: Love your enemies, do good to those who hate you, bless those who curse you, pray for those who mistreat you" (*Luke 6:27-28*). Even to those who have caused you pain, the Lord wants to turn you from thoughts of revenge to asking for His counsel. Regardless of the circumstances, God can deliver you from that potentially dangerous situation.

A man we'll identify as Norm lost his job when the computer company, where he had worked for seven years, merged with a major conglomerate and downsized. He was unable to find another job immediately so he decided to open a small software company. Three of his lifelong friends became investors and Norm launched the business in the basement of his home. After a few months, revenues grew to where he could afford to rent office space and hire another friend who had become unemployed. Several major contracts over a short period of time sent the business skyrocketing. He hired two more employees and moved to a larger building that would allow for future growth. The business was booming, and everyone was happy.

Then, Norm began depositing company money into a separate bank account that he kept secret from his partners. As the business continued to grow, so did his private bank account. Nearly 18 months passed before one of the investors questioned an item on the profit-and-loss statement — a contract for several thousand dollars recorded at a much lesser amount on the books. He called for an audit, and Norm's deception was unveiled. To experience the loss of trust and respect was far more painful to the lifelong investor friends than the loss of investment capital.

Pray the fourth part of Jabez's prayer — "*that I may not cause pain*" — as earnestly as the other words. The moments of sin that are often so small in our minds become everlasting pain to others.

HOW TO
AVOID CAUSING PAIN

1. Pray for God to give you words and actions that are pleasing to Him.

2. When you are angered, immediately ask the Lord to intervene.

3. Allow His power to work through you.

4. Exhort and encourage others.

5. Become like Jabez — a humble, kind servant of God.

> *"Brothers, if someone is caught in a sin, you who are spiritual should restore him gently. But watch yourself, or you also may be tempted."*

Galatians 6:1

Chapter Six

A SPIRITUAL
STRATEGIC PLAN

*"Teach us to number our days aright,
that we may gain a heart of wisdom."*

Psalms 90:12

Jabez, Inc.

A STRATEGIC PLAN is the blueprint by which corporations reach their objectives. There are four questions I ask corporate executives in a planning session:

1. *What* do we *really* do?
2. *How* do we do it?
3. For *whom* do we do it?
4. *Why* do we do it?

After several minutes of pondering these questions, they begin writing answers, erasing them, and writing again until they find words that will hopefully define their perceptions. From their answers to the four simple questions, we begin wordsmithing to create a vision statement of the new corporate horizon to be focused on in the next year, three years, five years and beyond.

Next on the planning agenda, we identify the key business drivers — things like products, customers, technology, equipment, advertising and marketing that sustain and propel the organization. Objective statements that describe the expected outcome for each of the business drivers are written; then milestones listing the key projects and events that must occur for the objectives to be reached, followed by specific goals and measurements to show progress; and finally, celebrations for reaching various achievements in the entire program. Creating a corporate strategic plan is a complex, time consuming and mentally exhausting project.

For years I asked only the first three questions in a strategic planning session. In 1998, I was facilitating a program for a major food company at a resort in Florida. The evening before the first session, I was introduced to the key executives, the last one being the marketing director. We shook hands and he asked me what I did for a living. "I work with companies to build a competitive advantage through stronger leadership, effective work teams and better customer service," I replied. He responded, "Why?" For the first time in my life, I was speechless. After a few moments, I finally uttered, "You know, I'm not quite sure. I'll have to think about it and get back to you with my answer."

His question continued to haunt me during dinner. I searched my mind for reasons why I travel great distances, stay in hotels, eat in restaurants, and work in unfamiliar places with people I've never met. Later that evening, I approached him to give him my answer:

"I'm from a farm community in Indiana. My Dad worked at a General Motors plant rather than become a farmer like many of his relatives. Like him, I had no interest in farming as a career. But I realize now that my job today is farming. Every day I sow seeds of information that help people become better employees, citizens, parents and spouses. These people plant, nourish and grow my seeds of improvement in their minds that eventually produce stronger leaders and productive human beings. My greatest reward is seeing people grow and reach their utmost potential. That's why I do what I do."

Have you ever thought about how these four questions and strategic planning apply to your life? *What* do you *really* do? Think about your job, your career, your family, your church and social activities — everything that consumes the 168 hours in your life each week.

Now, *how* do you do it? "Sometimes I wonder," is the typical reply. "With everything I have on my plate, it's a miracle I get through the week." Sound familiar? Everybody seems to be in the rut of too much to do with too little time. Next question: For *whom* do you do it? That's easy — you and your family, customers, business associates, etc., etc. Okay, final question: *Why* do you do it? Again, a typical answer: "Uh, well, I like to get paid for my job, and I love my family, and I need to pay bills, and . . ."

Like a corporation, we need to find answers to these questions to form our spiritual strategic plan for the future. Do you have one? Take a moment right now to write down your answers to the four questions that will lay a foundation on which you can create your personal spiritual plan.

> *What do you really do?* How productive are you? Do you utilize your time well? Do you take advantage of the opportunities that God provides for you to witness for Him? Is your life a living testimony for the Lord? How do you define your life's job description?

> *How do you do it?* Do you perform your job to the best of your ability? Are your motives ethical and honest? Are you trustworthy? In

your relationships, do you show compassion and consideration to others?

For whom do you do it? Stop for a moment and reflect on people outside your circle of family, friends and relatives. Think about the influence you have on others in your job — associates who work with you, employees in other departments, plants and geographic territories, leaders, customers, vendors and people you come in contact with during the course of each day. Your actions reflect your values, morals and principles.

Why do you do it? Search your soul for the answer. As a staff member of Jabez, Inc., your job is to be a connector, a messenger, a laborer for God, reaching out to serve others. Your ultimate reward is a fulfilling life that only the Lord can offer. Isn't that reason enough?

Jabez did not have a specific plan, but he knew that more blessings and bigger territory would require increased divine guidance and protection. He didn't have the advantage of creating his own spiritual strategic plan, but you can design one that will prepare you for your new job in His workforce. With your answers to the four previous questions in mind, begin now to write your plan.

> *Vision* — What is your vision of God? In the broad spectrum of life, is He the sole supplier of your needs; a Lord who owns and controls everything; One with whom you have an intimate relationship; your business partner, and a caring, compassionate God who loves you? Does His love penetrate your soul? Is he someone you communicate with daily in prayer? Is He the Alpha and Omega — truly the beginning and the end? Your vision of God is the foundation on which all other aspects of your strategic plan will be built. Now, consider these questions: What is God's vision of you? As CEO of Jabez, Inc., what position can He reserve for you? Can He honor you as he did Jabez? Complete this sentence: "My vision of God is . . ."

> *Key Spiritual Drivers* — What are the pillars that support your vision? For example, faith, God's

love, His promises, truth, prayer and eternal life are a few of the sustaining elements of the plan. What are your supportive columns?

Objectives — What do you hope to accomplish in each of your key drivers? Write your objective statements. For example:

> *Faith* — To place complete trust in Him through good times and bad.

> *God's love* — To be eternally grateful for the outpouring of undeserved blessings that come only from Him.

> *His promises* — To lean totally upon the Lord for every need knowing that He is my sole supplier.

> *Truth* — To know that His word never wavers — it's the constant absolute truth.

> *Prayer* — To communicate with the Lord offering praise and thanksgiving for our blessings and to seek His favor through the words of Jabez.

Milestones — Once your life is in alignment
with His purpose and your day-to-day activities
reflect the Lord's direction, miracles will happen.
Total dependence on Him for our needs allows
God to pour out blessings abundantly. The milestones in your life will become Jabez moments
when His love flows through you. Write the
actions you must initiate to make your objective
statements happen.

Goals — Goals are specific steps necessary to make milestones occur. As God answers your prayers for expanded territory, there will be many opportunities for you to become more involved in His works. In those situations, your goal might be to contribute a specific amount of time, labor and money. Make your goals SMART:

Specific — exactly what you plan to accomplish.

Measurements — establish checkpoints on where you plan to be at the end of the first week, second week, etc. toward achieving your goal.

Action steps — In detail, write each step you will take.

Resources — Are there resources (books, materials, time, money, etc.) you will need?

Time-base — Your goal must have a deadline, the date and time you plan to achieve your goal. Don't write "as soon as possible." When is that? Be definite.

I suggest setting a limit to 30-days on each goal. Beyond four weeks, people tend to lose momentum. Written goals are the motivators of our aspirations.

Measurements — Without measurements, we settle for mediocrity. Noting your progress in achieving goals and milestones outlined in the plan is important. Why else is a scoreboard necessary in an athletic event than to know where each team is at that specific point in the contest? Each team knows the score and what it will take to win. You need to know how well you are progressing in your plan. Remember, in Chapter One a 30-day journal was suggested to record God's blessings and to recognize the overflowing measure of love He sends forth.

Celebrations — Rejoice and be happy in the Lord at all times!!

God expects productivity and results from His workforce. "Do you see a man who excels in his work? He will serve before kings; he will not serve before obscure men" (_Proverbs 22:29_). The Oriental term *kaizen*, meaning continuous improvement, is well known in total quality management circles. In other words, what we do today could and should be improved tomorrow. God wants you to make the best use of your skills and abilities and to constantly improve. Creativity and innovation are just as vital in spiritual work as in your professional job. If your strategy isn't working, change it.

Now, get ready because when God answers your Jabez prayer, your skills and strategies will be tested. There will be some surprises. His plan might not coincide with your strategies. Be flexible and yield to His will. Stay on God's course and you will continue to receive blessings and power. The only detour will come through sin that constricts the flow of God's love and causes pain much deeper than any you have ever experienced before. Should that occur, reunite with the Lord immediately to ask forgiveness and restore the strength that only He can provide. "And God is able to make all grace abound to you, so that in all things at all times, having all that you need, you will abound in every good work" (*2 Corinthians 9:8*).

PROFIT/LOSS SHEET

LOSS	*GAIN*
God took our:	**God gave us His:**
Anxiety	Anointing
Brokenness	Blessing
Chastisement	Cleansing
Debts	Deliverance
Emptiness	Empowerment
Fears	Fullness
Guilt	Grace
Hopelessness	Holiness
Iniquity	Intercession
Judgment	Justification
Kingdom of darkness	Kingdom of light
Loneliness	Love
Mediocrity, mistakes	Mediation
Negativity	Nobility
Oppression	Overcoming power
Pain	Peace
Questioning	Quickening
Rejection	Redemption
Shame	Sanctification
Transgressions	Triumph
Unworthiness	Unmerited favor

Vices	Victory
Waywardness	Wisdom
eXcuses	eXample
Yoke of bondage	Yoke of discipleship
Zeal of the world	Zeal for God

"Wealth and honor come from You; You are the ruler of all things. In Your hands are strength and power to exalt and give strength to all."

1 Chronicles 29:12

Chapter Seven

HIS PRAYER
WAS ANSWERED

". . . and God granted his request."

❧

Jabez, Inc.

SOMETIMES A SIMPLE PRAYER is answered in the most profound way. The prayer of Jabez is not a long, itemized appeal, yet God heard his few words. There is very little background on Jabez other than he was more honorable than his brothers. I believe he must have been *a fast-paced, task-oriented man*, not concerned about details. In modern-day behavioral styles, he might be identified as a "D" for Dominant in the DISC model of human behavior taught by Dr. Robert Rohm and explained in his book *Positive Personality Profiles.*

Because of his name, Jabez probably had been snubbed. I imagine he sized up his lot in life and decided it was time to call for action. If Jabez was a purchasing agent today, his prayer might be: "God, I need a ton of blessings in a larger area. I want your guidance to keep me from evil and pain. Thank you, Lord." Short, to the point, a bottom-line approach — cut to the chase.

Several years ago at my small apartment in Nashville, Tennessee, I prayed a one-sentence prayer one night: "Lord, bring a Christian woman into my life." This occurred during a time in my life when I did not have a close relationship with God.

I thought the prayer probably hit the living room ceiling and bounced back. After a few months there, I returned to my native state of Indiana. One night, I received a phone call from an Army buddy inviting me to join his company in Atlanta. I accepted his offer and moved to an apartment at Lake Lanier, north of the city.

It was the one year anniversary of my move when a friend called one evening and invited me to join her and her friend at a restaurant where they were having dinner. It was 9 o'clock at night and I was not dressed appropriately. I could not be there for at least an hour and a half so, I graciously declined. Despite all my excuses, my friend finally convinced me.

At the restaurant, I was introduced to a lovely lady named Lynn. We began talking about our backgrounds, our experiences and things that people talk about on their first meeting. Later in the evening, I made some humorous remark, she laughed and impulsively touched my arm. At that moment, the warmth of her touch radiated through my body. It was not like a sudden bolt of electricity but a soothing sensation of tenderness.

No, I didn't suddenly blurt out, "You're the one for me!" I did realize, however, there was something special about her. We began dating and, a few months later Lynn became my wife. God granted my request for a Godly woman.

Why did He answer my simple prayer? I was not walking closely with the Lord. As a "lukewarm Christian," I prayed occasionally, usually when a need or crisis arose. And yet, He heard every one of those prayers. He was patient with me. The prayer for a Christian woman in my life, spoken with low expectation, went directly to Him. That's how God works. Regardless of your circumstances, He wants you to ask — in long prayers and short ones. The Lord withholds nothing from those who earnestly yearn for a "more honorable" designation in their lives.

Asking to be "more honorable" in God's view is not egotistical or conceited. To be declared "more honorable" is strictly up to Him, not a designation we can claim for ourselves. Striving to forge ahead of

another person to win His favor would be like someone trying to selfishly receive an unwarranted promotion. When your intentions are right, you're earnestly
opening your heart with strong faith and unlimited
expectations to seek God's highest tribute. The rewards
are a blessed life of Jabez Moments occurring at pre-
cisely the right time.

These are exciting times because opportunities
abound. John 4:35 says, "I tell you, open your eyes
and look at the fields! They are ripe for harvest."
Think what could happen if you volunteered to be
a one-person Jabez representative. Immediately God
becomes your partner with his resourcefulness and
empowerment. You rise above your talents and are
capable of doing more through His guidance. For
every person you meet, pray that the Lord will use
you. Look for opportunities where you can do
God's work.

Larry was the leader of a work team in a plant
where I was hired as a consultant. Each week, I would
meet with leaders to discuss their challenges in devel-
oping the new team building system. He was a quiet
individual who always appeared to be troubled. When

asked how things were going, Larry would reply, "Fine." But his facial expression and body language said otherwise.

He came in one day and seemed very sad, more so than in our previous meetings. Rather than ask my usual question about how his team was progressing, I asked him, "How are you doing?" His reply was the same as before, "Fine." I said, "Larry, I want to know how *you* are doing? I have a feeling something is really troubling you. Is there something I can help you with?"

He sat in silence for a few moments, tears welled up in his eyes and he started telling me about his situation. Larry and his wife had been married for seven years and they had two small children. For the past couple years, she had been drinking excessively and he suspected her of having an extramarital affair. He felt they had worked through many of their problems and were making progress. When he returned home from work one evening, his wife had packed her bags and left. A next-door neighbor had the children. Six weeks had passed and he had not heard from her. He was devastated.

I shared some personal experiences and how God had carried me through my troubled times. We prayed and I asked the Lord to bring peace to Larry. When he came in for our meeting the following week, his entire demeanor had changed. His heart still ached but he had peace. As the weeks continued and I talked with Larry, there was a noticeable change in his outlook. He had reunited with God.

Reflecting on this Jabez moment, I did not play the role of marriage councilor, advisor — or even God. I was simply a member of His workforce. He provided the right words for that moment. So often we fail to see the hurting world around us. There are countless people like Larry who are suffering from all kinds of problems who need His grace. They can experience His love through you. All you need to do is be available — just show up! He will give you the power to be His agent.

When the Lord sent Samuel to anoint one of Jesse's sons to be king, the least likely was chosen. Seven of his sons were considered but each time, God reminded Samuel that man looks at the outward appearance but He looks at the heart. "Are these all the sons you have?" Samuel asked Jesse. "There is still the youngest," Jesse answered, "but he is tending the sheep." Samuel said, "Send for him."

Jesse probably thought, "You've gotta be kidding. My youngest son David is only a shepherd. He likes music and writes poetry. You're gonna consider *him* to be *king*?" The Lord knew David's heart and chose to give him power to do His work. With a slingshot and stone, David carried out a "giant" assignment!

Like an employee in a new job, God will give you divine power to grow as you experience each Jabez moment. As you continue to pray, new blessings will come in a wider territory; more power will be given to you and His protection will be ever-present. You will experience a closer relationship with the Lord each day.

Remember the word *kaizen*, the Oriental term for continuous improvement? The Jabez lifestyle is one of continuous growth. You never stop praying for God to continue the flow of blessings so He can lead you into an even larger territory. He will help you grow each day in your Jabez journey.

Don't confuse the Jabez lifestyle with the land

of milk and honey. There will be tests of your faith. Opportunities will appear at work that will tempt you to turn away from your job with God. There will be doubts and fears. In these times, your commitment will be on the line. Are you really willing to yield to God — regardless of where He leads? This, as they say, is where the rubber meets the road. When you decide *His* purpose holds priority over your position, job, skills and salary, God will take great pleasure in honoring you as a dedicated staff member of Jabez, Inc.

ASKING FOR HONOR

1. Without seeking personal gain, pray for God to honor your requests.

2. Understand that it's His decision, not yours.

3. Don't become overwhelmed with the bounty of the Lord's blessings.

4. Continue praying daily for more blessings and territory.

5. Overcome temptations to avoid Jabez moments.

"No one can serve two masters. Either he will hate the one and love the other, or he will be devoted to the one and despise the other. You cannot serve both God and man."

Matthew 6:24

Chapter Eight

GOING TO WORK AT JABEZ, INC.

"You're hired!"

❧

Jabez, Inc.

REMEMBER WHEN YOU BEGAN a new job? Everything was different. Unfamiliar surroundings, new people, different ways of doing things — the whole scene was a bit uncomfortable and fearful. There have been times in my life when I left one job for another only to wish the first day I was back in my old slot. It was frightening!

Are you ready to join God's workforce and begin work at Jabez, Inc.? There's no application to fill out, no interview, no screening and no waiting for a vacancy to occur. You simply volunteer and then show up for your assignment. This job is unlike any other you've ever held. Let's look at the differences here compared to the business world:

1. The employee manual is the Bible. All the rules, regulations, policies and procedures are outlined from Genesis to Revelation. If you are ever in doubt, pray and check the scriptures for correct direction, guidance and advice.

2. The training program calls for you to make the

prayer of Jabez an addition to your daily prayer life, not a replacement. Begin each day with a sincere request for God to increase His blessings, widen your territory, keep his hand of guidance upon you, protect you from evil and prevent you from causing pain.

3. You will have an open job description. There will not be a daily routine of specific duties. The tasks will vary from day to day at His choosing. But, be assured, He will not ask you to do anything without His full support. Incidentally, your hours are 24/7.

4. The authority to perform your duties will be from the Lord. He will be the sole provider of strength and power to perform any task requested and overcome all challenges. As you continue in your job, His strength and power will be increased.

5. Keep a daily journal of God's blessings. At the end of each day, reflect on the blessings you've received. Be prepared to expand your journal as He gives you more and more.

6. As your attitude and willingness to serve in Jabez, Inc. grows, be prepared to handle more assign-

ments — with an increase in blessings, eagerly given in love. There will be no power struggles or office politics to consider.

7. Resist temptations that might detract from your responsibilities as a staff member. You'll face competition, challenges and resistance as more of God's power is given to you. There will be distractions, diversions, disruptions and all kinds of devilish deceptions to keep you from performing your job. Ignore all attempts!

8. Be "on call" at any time for God to issue an order. Some will be obvious, others may seem unusual and there could be some that appear impossible. Regardless, follow His directions. You will experience miracles!

9. Benefits include the best spiritual lifestyle, superb insurance protection, guaranteed promotion, and special honors from the Jabez, Inc. CEO for obedience. He loves to give. All you need to do is have faith and ask.

10. Job security is assured and new territory is awarded upon request. And your retirement plan is out of this world!

Are you ready to go to work? There's excitement in the air because the veterans of Jabez, Inc., those who have already experienced God's bountiful blessings, know what's in store for you. They know the transformation that takes place in the hearts of people when they begin receiving all He has to offer. An overwhelming feeling of gratitude and wonder brings them to tears as they see the miracles that God performs through each one. They welcome new members and rejoice as the Jabez, Inc. workforce expands.

The Lord is asking you to rely on Him alone. God will test you but His testing is not so He can see what _you_ are made of. Rather, it is so you can know what _you_ are made of to face fear and doubt. And, at the same time, you can know what _He_ is made of —being faithful, trustworthy, merciful and mindful of you! By completely trusting God, your life will be filled with abundant joy.

No job in any worldly company — large, midsize or small — can compare! Every corporation has people who lead and those who follow. My definition of a leader is one who gets people (followers) to willingly do the work that must be done. At Jabez, Inc. each person is both leader and follower: A leader to bring others willingly to the Lord and a faithful follower of Him.

Are you ready to fill that job?

At the beginning of this book, I revealed how incapable I felt when the idea of writing *Jabez, Inc.* was presented to me. Putting my faith in God, I depended on Him to supply the words. Next came the time factor. When would I find time to write? My schedule is usually filled with speaking engagements and seminar dates. As I looked at my calendar, there were several open days. God knew long before *Jabez, Inc.* was suggested that I would need time at my computer keyboard for us to work together. He has supplied everything!

As the final words are written for this book, I'm preparing to pack my bags and resume a busy schedule again. I'll be speaking and conducting seminars in the corporate world but, at the same time, I'll be a Jabez, Inc. staff member serving God wherever he sends me.

Will you join me for that joyous adventure!

God will be well pleased.

"*Do not conform any longer to the pattern of this world, but be transformed by the renewing of your   mind. Then you will be able to test and approve what God's will is — his good, pleasing and perfect will.*"

Romans 12:2

GENE SWINDELL is a veteran speaker and seminar leader who has appeared before thousands in presentations throughout the United States and 16 other countries around the globe. Known as the *Voice of Change*™, he speaks on personal development, leadership, team building and customer service topics.

His voice has been the trademark for much of his career. Starting as a reporter at small newspapers, he moved on to radio as a disc jockey, announcer and news director and later became a television news anchorman and host. His voice and face have been featured in over 100 radio and television commercials as well as many corporate training programs. Today, Swindell hosts the syndicated radio show *The Voice of Change* and appears as guest commentator on radio and television business shows.

He has produced cassettes on leadership, customer service and professional telephone skills and has written *The New ABCs of Success* and articles for major business publications.

Listed in the worldwide *Who's Who in Professional*

Speaking and *Who's Who in Sales and Marketing*,
Swindell is a member of the National Speakers Association, American Society for Training and Development,
Meeting Planners International and American Society
of Association Executives. He has been awarded Speaker
of the Year by the National Speakers Association.

Gene is President of Creative Concepts International,
Inc., in Atlanta, GA. He works with companies to form
strong organizations with quality leadership and effective
teams to create a competitive advantage in the marketplace. His client list reads like a *Who's Who in Business*.